SAS ODBC Driver Tec Report: User's Guide and Programmer's Reference

Release 6.11

SAS Institute Inc.
SAS Campus Drive
Cary, NC 27513

Contents

Using This Book

Purpose and Audience

This report documents the Release 6.11 version of the SAS ODBC driver. If you are using the Release 6.10 version of the driver, you should refer to *SAS ODBC Driver Technical Report: User's Guide and Programmer's Reference,* **Release 6.10** The main difference between the two versions is that most of the SAS ODBC driver dialogs have been changed. See Chapter 2, "Defining Your Data Sources," for more information.

This report is intended for three audiences:

☐ users who are using the SAS ODBC driver to access data that are stored on their own computers.*

☐ system administrators who are using the SAS ODBC driver to enable multiple users to access shared data.

☐ applications programmers and others who need detailed information about how the SAS ODBC driver has been implemented.

In this report, we assume that all readers are familiar with the Microsoft Windows, Windows NT, or Windows for Workgroups operating environments and that they know how to use the mouse and keyboard to perform common Windows tasks.

Additional Documentation

The following sections list documentation that may be useful to you when you use the SAS ODBC driver.

SAS Documentation

SAS Institute provides many publications about products of the SAS System and how to use them in particular operating environments. For a complete list of SAS publications, refer to the current *Publications Catalog.* The catalog is produced twice a year. You can order a free copy of the catalog by writing, calling, or faxing the Institute:

> SAS Institute Inc.
> Book Sales Department
> SAS Campus Drive
> Cary, NC 27513
> Telephone: 919-677-8000
> Fax: 919-677-4444
> E-mail: sasbook@unx.sas.com

---

* See "What Kinds of Data Can I Access with the SAS ODBC Driver?" on page 2 for information about what kinds of data you can access.

SAS/ACCESS Software Documentation

The SAS/ACCESS interface guides explain how to use SAS/ACCESS software with other software vendors' products. For a complete list of SAS/ACCESS interface guides, consult the *Publications Catalog* .

□ *Getting Started with SAS/ACCESS Software, Version 6, First Edition* (order #A55103) uses tutorials to show you how to create and edit access descriptors and view descriptors. It also shows you how to insert data into a database table and how to use the SQL Procedure Pass-Through facility. Tutorials and examples use data from SAS/ACCESS interfaces to relational database management systems and to PC file formats.

□ *SAS/ACCESS Software for Relational Databases: Reference, Version 6, First Edition* (order #A55144). This book is bound in a three-ring binder and must be used in conjunction with a DBMS chapter. DBMS chapters are ordered separately and can be inserted into the binder:

   □ AS/400 Data Chapter (order #A55155)

   □ DB2 Chapter (order #A55145)

   □ DB2/2 Chapter (order #A55142)

   □ DEC Rdb Chapter (order #A55161)

   □ INGRES Chapter (order #A55133)

   □ ORACLE Chapter (order #A55226)

   □ SQL/DS Chapter (order #A55194)

   □ SYBASE and SQL Server Chapter (order #A55310)

□ *SAS/ACCESS Interface to ADABAS: Usage and Reference, Version 6, First Edition* (order #A56065)

□ *SAS/ACCESS Interface to CA-DATACOM/DB: Usage and Reference, Version 6, First Edition* (order #A56066)

□ *SAS/ACCESS Interface to CA-IDMS: Reference, Version 6, First Edition* (order #A55180)

□ *SAS/ACCESS Interface to IMS-DL/I: Usage and Reference, Version 6, Second Edition* (order #A55270)

□ *SAS/ACCESS Software for PC File Formats: Reference, Version 6, First Edition* (order #A55206)

□ *SAS/ACCESS Interface to SYSTEM 2000 Data Management Software: Usage and Reference, Version 6, First Edition* (order #A56064)

□ *SAS/ACCESS Software Changes and Enhancements: SQL Procedure Pass-Through Facility, Version 6* (order #A55237). This report includes information about how to access data from various sources, such as ODBC, DB2/6000, Informix, ORACLE, and SYBASE and SQL Server. Because the Pass-Through facility uses a SAS/ACCESS interface view engine to connect to data sources other than with the SAS System, you must have a license for one of the SAS/ACCESS interfaces in order to use the facility.

SAS Operating System Companions

The SAS Companions provide operating system-specific information about basic tasks such as accessing and using SAS files, using external files, and routing output. They also describe how to use the SAS System to its fullest in specific operating environments.

☐ *SAS Companion for the CMS Environment, Version 6, First Edition* (order #A56103)

☐ *SAS Companion for the Microsoft Windows Environment, Version 6, First Edition* (order #A56110)

☐ *SAS Companion for the Microsoft Windows NT Environment, Version 6, First Edition* (order #A56112)

☐ *Microsoft Windows Environment: Changes and Enhancements to the SAS System, Release 6.10* (order #55107)

☐ *SAS Companion for the MVS Environment, Version 6, First Edition* (order #A56101)

☐ *SAS Companion for the OS/2 Environment, Version 6, Second Edition* (order #A56111)

☐ *OS/2 Environment: Changes and Enhancements to the SAS System, Release 6.10* (order #A55137)

☐ *SAS Companion for UNIX Environments: User Interfaces, Version 6, First Edition* (order #A56113)

☐ *SAS Companion for UNIX Environments: Language, Version 6, First Edition* (order #A56114)

☐ *SAS Companion for the VMS Environment, Version 6, First Edition* (order #A56102)

☐ *SAS Companion for the VSE Environment, Version 6, First Edition* (order #A56109)

The SAS System's SQL Procedure

If your Windows application requires you to use Structured Query Language (SQL) statements to query your data sources, then you may need information about how the SAS System's SQL procedure implements SQL under Version 6 of the SAS System.

☐ *SAS Guide to the SQL Procedure: Usage and Reference, Version 6, First Edition* (order #A56070)

☐ *Getting Started with the SQL Procedure, Version 6, First Edition* (order #A55042)

☐ *SAS Technical Report P-254, Using the SQL Query Window, Release 6.08* (order #A59171)

SAS/SHARE Software

SAS/SHARE software includes a server that the SAS ODBC driver uses to access remote SAS data sources.

☐ *SAS/SHARE Software: Usage and Reference, Version 6, First Edition* (order #A56014)

☐ *SAS/SHARE Technical Report for the Microsoft Windows Environment, Release 6.11* (order #A55330)

☐ *SAS/SHARE Technical Report for the OS/2 Environment, Release 6.11* (order #A55332)

☐ *SAS/SHARE Technical Report for UNIX Environments, Release 6.11* (order #A55331)

□ SAS Technical Report P-260, *SAS/SHARE Software for the MVS Environment, Release 6.08* (order #A59177)

□ SAS Technical Report P-261, *SAS/SHARE Software for the CMS Environment, Release 6.08* (order #A59178)

□ SAS Technical Report P-265, *SAS/SHARE Software for the OpenVMS Environment, Releases 6.08 and 6.09* (order #A55197)

□ SAS Technical Report P-267, *SAS/SHARE Software for the VSE Environment, Release 6.08* (order #A55321)

Microsoft ODBC Documentation

Applications programmers and others who need detailed information about Microsoft's ODBC specification should consult the following document:

□ *Microsoft ODBC 2.0 Programmer's Reference and SDK Guide*

Other ODBC Documentation

Refer to the documentation provided with your Windows application for additional information about accessing data with an ODBC driver.

Chapter 1 Introducing the SAS® ODBC Driver

What is ODBC?

ODBC stands for Open Database Connectivity. It is an interface standard that provides a common application programming interface (API) for accessing databases. Many software products that run in the Windows operating environment adhere to this standard, giving users access to data that were created with other software.

ODBC functionality is provided by three main components: the client application, the ODBC driver manager, and the ODBC driver (see Figure 1.1). The ODBC driver manager, which was developed by Microsoft, manages the interaction between a client application and one or more ODBC drivers.

What is the SAS ODBC Driver?

The SAS ODBC driver is an implementation of the ODBC standard that enables you to access, manipulate, and update SAS data sources from ODBC-compliant applications. As Figure 1.1 shows, the SAS ODBC driver uses a SAS server to access data from your SAS data sources. The SAS server executes in an iconified, interactive SAS session. (See "SAS Servers" on page 5 for more information). If you use other ODBC drivers (such as those for ORACLE or SQL Server) to access other data sources, those drivers may require additional software components.

Note: To access ODBC data sources from within the SAS System (the opposite of what the SAS ODBC driver enables you to accomplish), you must license the SAS/ACCESS interface to ODBC, which is documented in *SAS/ACCESS Software Changes and Enhancements: SQL Procedure Pass-Through Facility, Version 6.*

Figure 1.1
Components of
ODBC Functionality

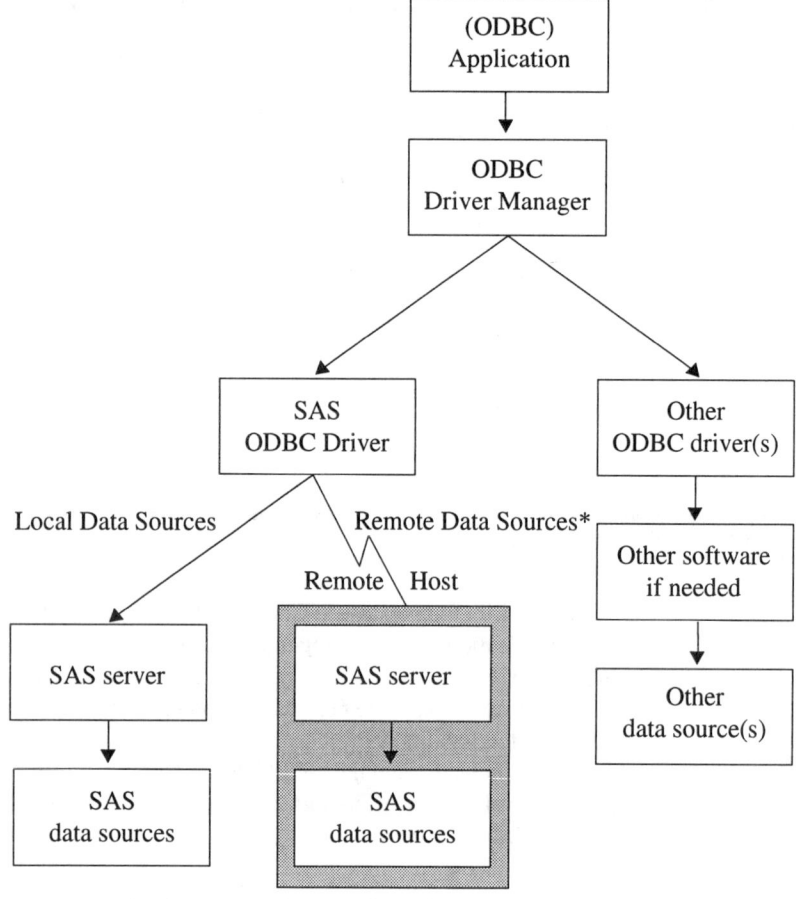

*To access remote data sources, the SAS ODBC driver requires communications software (either TCP/IP or Network DDE). You must also license SAS/SHARE and SAS/SHARE*NET on the remote host.

What Kinds of Data Can I Access with the SAS ODBC Driver?

In Figure 1.1 and elsewhere throughout this report, we use the term *SAS data sources* to mean data sources that you have defined to the SAS ODBC driver. These can include not only SAS data sets, but also flat files and VSAM files, as well as data from many database management systems (DBMSs) through the use of SAS/ACCESS software. (See "SAS Data Sets" on page 3 for details.)

If your PC is on a network, you can access both local data sources and remote data sources. (See "What Software Do I Need?" on page 6 for information about software requirements.) *Local data* are data that you access through a SAS server on your machine. The data may be stored either on your PC hard drive or on a PC network file system, such as a Novell file server, that makes the physical location of the data transparent to applications. *Remote data* are data that you access through a SAS server that is running on another machine.

The ability to use the SAS ODBC driver in conjunction with SAS/ACCESS software as a gateway to DBMS data is particularly useful under any of the following circumstances:

□ There is no ODBC driver for the remote DBMS. Therefore, you use the SAS ODBC driver in conjunction with SAS/ACCESS software in the remote SAS server to get ODBC connectivity.

□ You don't have a license for the necessary software (either an ODBC driver for the DBMS or DBMS network access software) on your client machine.

□ You want to join or merge DBMS data with other data on a remote host.

Currently, SAS/ACCESS software is available for the following:

ADABAS	DB2/6000	PC File Formats*
AS/400 Data	DEC Rdb	SQL/DS
CA-DATACOM/DB	IMS-DL/I	SQL Server
CA-IDMS	Informix	SYBASE
DB2	INGRES	System 2000
DB2/2	ORACLE	

For information about the individual SAS/ACCESS interfaces, see the documentation listed in "SAS/ACCESS Software Documentation" on page iv.

What Do I Need to Know about the SAS System?

To use the SAS ODBC driver, you need to understand three components of the SAS System:

□ SAS data sets

□ SAS data libraries

□ SAS servers.

You also need to understand the correspondence between ODBC terminology and SAS terminology. These topics are explained in the following sections.

SAS Data Sets

A SAS data set is a file that the SAS System can access as if it were a physical object containing the following:

□ data values that are stored in tabular form

□ a descriptor portion that defines the types of data to the SAS System.

The physical locations of the data values and the descriptor are not necessarily contiguous.
    SAS data sets have two forms: data *files* and data *views*. SAS data *files* are essentially relational tables with columns (or variables) and rows (or observations). The SAS data file structure can have many of the characteristics of a database management system, including

---

*   includes DBF, DIF, WK1, WK3, WK4, and XLS file formats.

indexing, compression, and password protection.

SAS data *views* are definitions or descriptions of data that reside elsewhere. They enable you to use the SAS System to access many different data sources, including flat files, VSAM files, and DBMS structures, as well as native SAS data files. They also eliminate the need for users to know anything about the structure of the data or the software that was used to create it.

Because they contain no data, views take up very little storage. And because they collect the actual data values only when called, they always access the most current data from their defined sources.

Views can be used to define subsets of larger structures, or supersets of data that have been enhanced with calculated values. You can also create SAS data views that combine views of dissimilar data sources. For example, a view of a relational DB2 table can be combined with a view of a SAS data file, a view of hierarchical IMS-DL/I data, or even a view from a PC-based dBASE file.

You can create SAS data views in three ways:

□ with the DATA step (DATA step views)

□ with the SQL procedure (PROC SQL views)

□ with the ACCESS procedure (SAS/ACCESS views).

There is some variation among these types of views, as described in the following table.

Table 1.1
Types of SAS Data
Views

Type of View	Description
DATA step views	can describe data from one or more sources, including flat files, VSAM files, and SAS data sets (either files or other views). Because a DATA step view only *reads* other files, you cannot use it to update the view's underlying data. For more information about creating and using DATA step views, see Chapter 14, "Input DATA Step Views," in *SAS Technical Report P-222, Changes and Enhancements to Base SAS Software, Release 6.07.*
PROC SQL views	can define either a subset or a superset of data from one or more SAS data sets (either files or views, including views that are created with the PROC SQL Pass-Through facility to access DBMS data). For example, the SQL procedure can combine data from PROC SQL views, DATA step views, and SAS/ACCESS views with data in a SAS data file. You cannot use PROC SQL views to update the data in the view's underlying files or tables. However, with some restrictions, you can use the UPDATE, DELETE, and INSERT statements in the SQL procedure to update data that are described by SAS/ACCESS views. For more information, see Chapter 3, "Creating and Modifying Tables and Views," in *SAS Guide to the SQL Procedure: Usage and Reference.* For information about the PROC SQL Pass-Through facility, see the documentation for the SAS/ACCESS interfaces that support this facility.

(continued)

Table 1.1
(continued)

Type of View	Description
SAS/ACCESS views	are created with the ACCESS procedure of SAS/ACCESS software. They are generally called *view descriptors* to distinguish them from PROC SQL or DATA step views. You can use them to describe data from any DBMS for which you license a SAS/ACCESS interface (see the list in "What Kinds of Data Can I Access with the SAS ODBC Driver?" on page 2). Each view descriptor describes all or some of the data in one DBMS table or in one DBMS view. When the SAS servers that are used by the SAS ODBC driver are involved, most SAS/ACCESS interfaces do not permit you to use a view descriptor to update the underlying DBMS data. For more information about view descriptors, see your SAS/ACCESS documentation.

SAS Data Libraries

SAS data sets are contained in data libraries. Each SAS data library has two names: a physical name and a logical name (*libref*). The physical name of the library fully identifies the directory, filetype or minidisk, or host system data structure that contains the data sets. It must therefore conform to the rules for naming files within your host system.

You use the libref to identify a group of data sets (files or views) to the SAS System. The libref is a temporary name that you associate with the physical name of the SAS data library during each SAS job or session. After the libref is assigned, you can read, create, or update files in the data library. A libref is valid only for the current SAS job or session and can be referenced repeatedly within that job or session.

For more information about SAS data libraries, see Chapter 31, "SAS Data Libraries," in *SAS Language and Procedures, Version 6, First Edition.*

SAS Servers

To access your SAS data sources, the SAS ODBC driver uses a *SAS server*. A SAS server is a SAS procedure (either PROC SERVER or PROC ODBCSERVER) that runs in its own SAS session; it accepts input and output requests from other SAS sessions and from the SAS ODBC driver on behalf of the ODBC-compliant application. While the server is running, the SAS session does not accept input from the keyboard.

The type of server that the driver uses depends on whether you are accessing local data or remote data:

local data	The driver uses a SAS ODBC server to access your data. If you do not already have a SAS session running on your PC, the driver starts a SAS session and executes PROC ODBCSERVER, thereby automatically starting the server for you when you connect to your local data source. See "Using DDE as Your Local Access Method" on page 24 for more information. If you have a SAS session (but not a SAS ODBC server)

(local data continued)

running on your PC, then you must either start the SAS ODBC server manually or end the SAS session before connecting to your SAS data sources.* See "Starting a SAS ODBC Server" on page 25 for details.

remote data   The driver uses a SAS/SHARE server. This requires that you license the SAS/SHARE*NET facility and SAS/SHARE software on the remote host. The driver also requires either TCP/IP or Network DDE software in order to communicate with the server. Your server administrator uses PROC SERVER to start the server on your remote host. See "Using TCP/IP as Your Remote Access Method" on page 25 and "Using Network DDE as Your Remote Access Method" on page 26 for more information.

SAS Terminology

Different software products often include similar components or constructs that are known by different names. For the ODBC standard and the SAS System, the following correspondences exist:

ODBC term	SAS term
owner	library name (libref)
table	data set
qualifier	not used

Therefore, if your ODBC-compliant application asks you to specify the owner for a SAS data library, you should specify the libref. If the application asks for a table name, supply the name of the SAS data set. If a qualifier is requested, you can generally leave the field blank.

What Software Do I Need?

The SAS ODBC driver runs under Release 3.1 or later of Windows, Windows NT, or Windows for Workgroups. It is available with Release 6.10 or later of the SAS System. **
    Other software requirements depend on your hardware configuration and on the data source(s) that you want to access, as shown in Table 1.2.

---

*   except under Windows NT, which supports multiple concurrent SAS sessions.
**   In Release 6.11, the principal SAS ODBC driver setup dialogs have been changed. Chapter 2 of this report reflects these changes.

Table 1.2
Software
Requirements

Data Source(s)	Configuration	Requirements
local SAS data only	Stand-alone PC	Base SAS*
local SAS data and local DBMS data	Stand-alone PC	Base SAS* SAS/ACCESS interface for each DBMS
remote SAS data	PC on a network	On PC: SAS ODBC driver*** TCP/IP** or Network DDE On remote host: Base SAS SAS/SHARE SAS/SHARE*NET TCP/IP** or Network DDE
remote SAS data and remote DBMS data	PC on a network	On PC: SAS ODBC driver*** TCP/IP** or Network DDE On remote host: Base SAS SAS/SHARE SAS/SHARE*NET SAS/ACCESS interface for each DBMS TCP/IP** or Network DDE

* For local data access, base SAS software includes the SAS ODBC driver, but you install the driver separately.
** Requires a version of TCP/IP that supports the Microsoft Windows socket ("winsock") API.
*** For remote data access, the SAS ODBC driver is included with SAS/SHARE*NET. You install the driver on your client PCs, and you use the SAS SETINIT to enable SAS/SHARE*NET on the remote host.

Chapter 2 Defining Your Data Sources

Introduction

After you install the SAS ODBC driver,* you must provide information about the data source(s) that you want to access. This chapter explains how to use the SAS ODBC driver dialog boxes to provide the necessary information.

From the SAS ODBC dialogs, you can select **Help** at any time to obtain information about the active dialog.

Accessing the SAS ODBC Driver Dialogs

To access the SAS ODBC dialogs, do the following:

1. From the Microsoft Windows (or Windows NT or Windows for Workgroups) Program Manager window, find the ODBC or ODBC Administrator icon. This icon may be located in the Control Panel group, in an ODBC group, or, if you have installed a package of other ODBC drivers, it may be in a group that is associated with that package.

2. Double-click on the icon. The Data Sources dialog appears. If you have not previously defined any data sources, then the **Data Sources [Driver]** listbox will be empty.

---

* See the installation instructions that are shipped with the driver diskette.

Display 2.1
Data Sources
Dialog

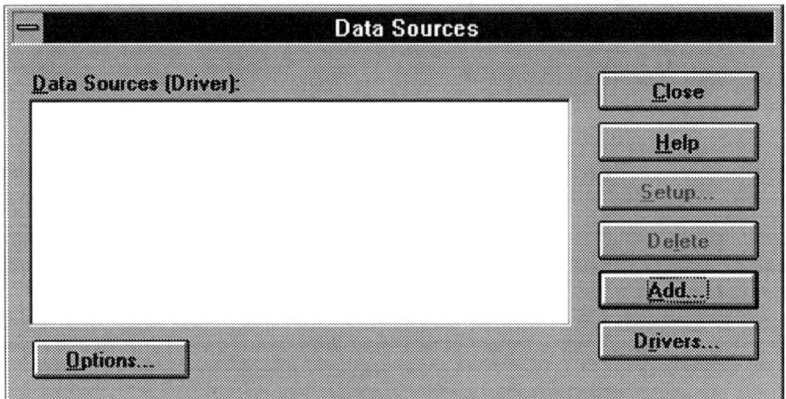

3. Select the **Add...** button on the right side of the dialog. The Add Data Source dialog appears.

Display 2.2
Add Data Source
Dialog

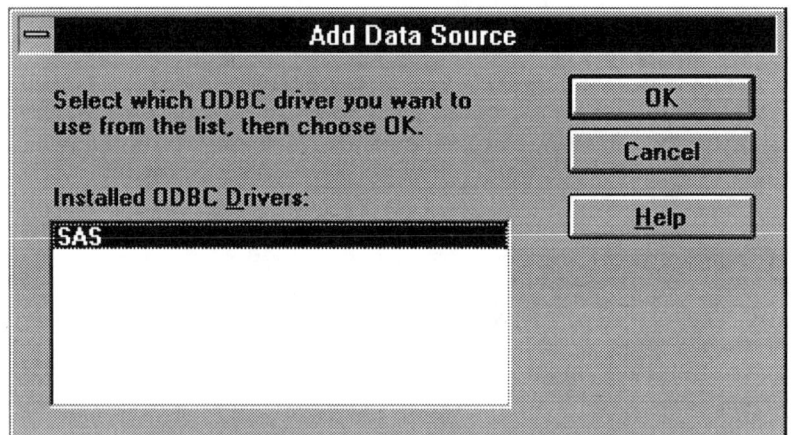

4. Scroll down in the list of Installed ODBC Drivers (if necessary) and double-click on **SAS**, or click once on **SAS** and then select **OK**.

    Note: You select **SAS** even if you are going to use a SAS data view to access non-SAS data. See "SAS Data Sets" on page 3 for information about SAS data views.

    The SAS ODBC Driver Configuration dialog appears (Display 2.3).

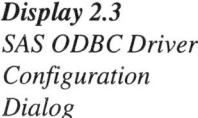

Display 2.3
SAS ODBC Driver
Configuration
Dialog

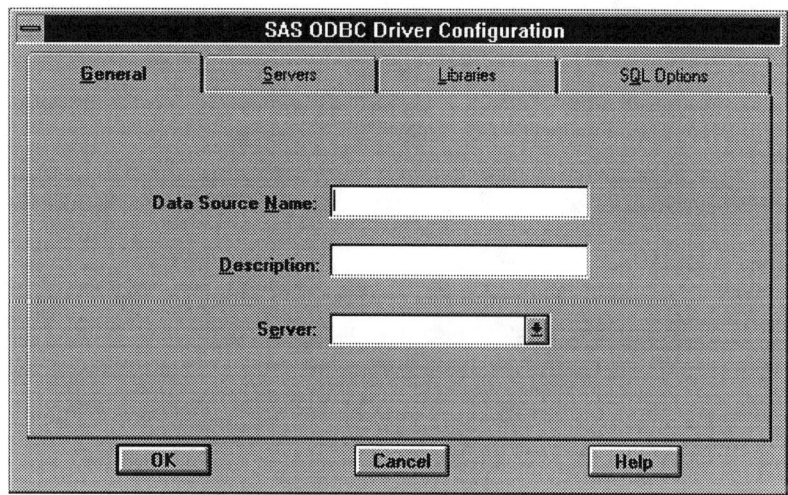

At the top of this dialog are four tabs—General, Servers, Libraries, and SQL Options. You select these tabs to move from one dialog page to the next. In each page you supply information about the data source that you want to be able to access.

After you have supplied all the necessary information, select the **OK** button from any page to save your data source definition. Selecting **Cancel** discards any new or changed information that you have supplied and returns you to the Data Sources dialog (Display 2.1).

Naming Your Data Source and Server

When you first access the SAS ODBC Driver Configuration dialog, the General page is at the foreground, as shown in Display 2.3.

1. In the **Data Source Name** field, enter a name for the data source that you want to access. The name must begin with a letter, and it cannot contain commas, semicolons, or any of the following special characters: **[ ] ( ) ? * = ! @** . For example, if you are defining SAS data that are stored on a machine named **CICERO**, you might call your data source **SAS_CICERO**. If you or other users are concerned only with the type of data (or with the type of application that uses that data), and not with where the data are stored, then you might have data sources with names like **Finance** or **Payroll**.

2. (Optional) In the **Description** field, you can supply a description of the data source.

3. The **Server** field has a drop-list icon next to it that you select in order to expand the list of defined servers. The first time you define a data source, the list is empty. Define one or more servers (as described in the next section), and then come back to the General page to make a selection from the Server list. You must specify a server for every data source.

Defining Servers

The SAS ODBC driver uses a SAS server to access your data sources. To access local data, the driver uses a SAS ODBC server. To access remote data, it uses a SAS/SHARE server. (See "SAS Servers" on page 5 for more information.)

This section explains how to provide the SAS ODBC driver with necessary information about the server(s) you will be using.

1. Select the **Servers** tab in the SAS ODBC Driver Configuration dialog to move the Servers page to the foreground. Supply the information described in the following steps. If at any point you want to clear all of the fields on the right side of the dialog and start again, select the **Clear** button in the upper right corner.

Display 2.4
Servers Page

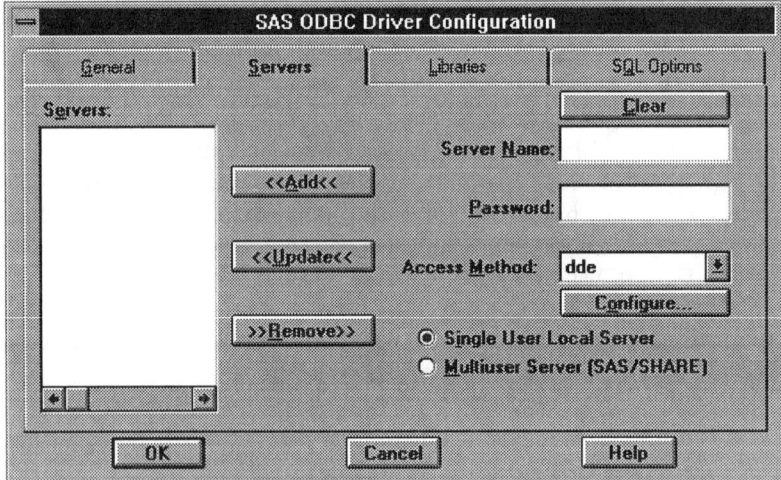

2. In the **Server Name** field, enter a name for the SAS server that you are defining. If you supply a one-part name such as **server1**, the SAS ODBC driver infers that the server is local. If you supply a two-part name such as **lamb.shr1**, the driver infers that the server is remote. For remote servers, the following rules also apply:

    □   If you are using TCP/IP to access remote data sources, then the driver interprets the first part of the name as a node name and the second part as the server name. The server name must match both the **ID=** field in PROC SERVER (the SAS/SHARE server that is running on the remote host), and the *server-name* that you (or your server administrator) specified when you defined the server as a service in the TCP/IP SERVICES file. See "Using TCP/IP as Your Remote Access Method" on page 25 for more information.

    □   If you are using Network DDE to access remote data, then the first part of the name must be the computer name of your remote Network DDE machine. The second part of the name must match the *share-name* that was used when you (or your server administrator) defined the DDE share. See "Using Network DDE as Your Remote Access Method" on page 26 for more information.

3. If user access to the server is password protected, then enter the password in the **Password** field. This should be the same password that was specified for the **UAPW=** option in PROC SERVER (for a SAS/SHARE server), or in PROC ODBCSERVER (for a local access server).

4. Select the drop-list icon that is next to the **Access Method** field, and select the appropriate access method from the list that appears. (This list is generated when you install the SAS ODBC driver. At present, TCP/IP and Network DDE are supported for access to remote data sources, and DDE is supported for access to local data sources. Select DDE if you want to specify either DDE or Network DDE.)
   Note: SAS is not a DDE server; it merely uses the DDE Management Library (DDEML) API as an access method for passing data to other ODBC-compliant applications.

5. If the server is a SAS ODBC server (used to access local data sources), then be sure that the **Single User Local Server** radio button is selected. If the server is a SAS/SHARE server (used by multiple users), select the **Multi-user Server [SAS/SHARE]** radio button.

6. Select the **Configure...** button. A dialog appears for the access method that you selected.

   □ If you selected DDE, but specified a two-part server name in the **Name** field of the Servers page (Display 2.4), then the SAS ODBC driver infers that you are using Network DDE to access a remote SAS/SHARE server. There are no configuration options for Network DDE, so a notification window simply informs you that the Network DDE server has been configured. Select **OK** to continue.

   □ If you selected DDE, but specified a one-part server name in the **Name** field of the Servers page (Display 2.4), then the SAS ODBC driver infers that you are using DDE to access a local SAS server. The Local DDE Options dialog appears.

Display 2.5
Local DDE Options
Dialog

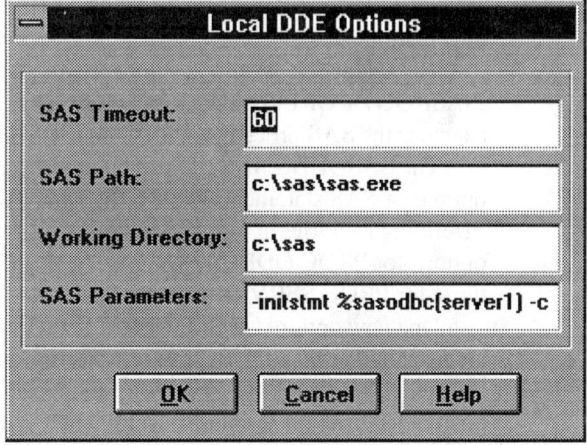

When you access a local SAS data source from an ODBC-compliant application, the SAS ODBC driver uses the information in this dialog to invoke a SAS ODBC server, provided there isn't one already running. (If a SAS ODBC server is already running, the driver finds it and connects to it.) Each field contains default values that you can change by typing over them.

SAS Timeout:
This option specifies in seconds how long to wait for the local SAS ODBC server to start and to register itself as a DDE server. The default is 60 seconds.

SAS Path:
Specify the fully qualified path name for the SAS executable file (SAS.EXE) that you use to start a SAS session. The default is **c:\sas\sas.exe**. If this field is empty, then no attempt is made to start a SAS ODBC server when you connect to your data source.

Working Directory:
Specify the fully qualified path name for the directory that you want to use as the SAS working directory. This directory is usually where your SAS program files and documents are located. The default is **c:\sas**.

SAS Parameters:
This field specifies the parameters that are used to invoke the SAS System. The default values are as follows: The initialization statement (**-initstmt**) executes a SAS macro (**%sasodbc**), which in turn invokes the ODBC server. The **server1** value is only an example. It is a SAS macro parameter whose value is taken from the name that you specified in the **Name** field of the Servers page (Display 2.4). The **-comamid dde** option (not fully visible in Display 2.5) specifies that the server will use DDE as its communications access method. The **-icon** option (not shown) specifies that the server session should be invoked in iconified mode, because no interaction with the server is required. The **-nologo** option (not shown) specifies that the SAS session will be invoked without displaying the SAS System logo and copyright information.

The **%sasodbc** macro is shipped with the SAS System and is found in !SASROOT\CORE\SASMACRO\SASODBC.SAS.* The SASODBC.SAS file executes the SAS procedure PROC ODBCSERVER.

The SASODBC.SAS file can be modified to add additional SAS system options or SAS statements such as the LIBNAME statements mentioned in "Defining Libraries at Server Startup Time" on page 18. You can also specify options for PROC ODBCSERVER. The available options are the same as those for PROC SERVER. See the SAS/SHARE documentation for details.

One new option, LOG=QUERY, is particularly relevant for servers that are used by the SAS ODBC driver. This option causes the server to log SQL queries. (By default, the server logs update and output operations, but not queries.) Hence, this option is useful when you need to see the queries that the server receives from an ODBC client application.

---

* !SASROOT is a logical name for the directory in which you install the SAS System. For more information, see the SAS documentation for the Microsoft Windows or Microsoft Windows NT operating environment.

If your SAS session is installed on a network drive and is shared by multiple users, then you probably don't want individual users to modify the SASODBC.SAS file. Instead, users can make their own copies of the file and can store them in their personal libraries. In this case, they must also add the **-sasautos** option either to the **SAS Parameters** field or to their local CONFIG.SAS file to indicate the path name for the library, as in the following example:

```
-sasautos c:\programs\sas
```

For more information about SAS system options and SAS statements, see the SAS documentation for the Microsoft Windows or Microsoft Windows NT operating environment.

□ If you selected TCP as your access method in the Servers page before selecting the **Configure...** button, the TCP Options dialog appears.

Display 2.6
TCP Options Dialog

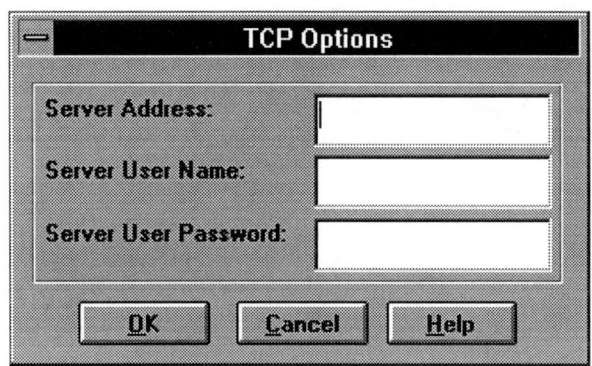

Supply the requested information in the dialog as follows:

Server Address:
This field is automatically filled with the node name that you specified in the **Name** field of the Servers page (Display 2.4). In a complex networking environment, you may need to supply a fully qualified domain address for the server (for example, **lamb.sas.com**).

Server User Name:
This field is for your userid on the system where the server is running. It is required if the server is running in secured mode; otherwise, it is ignored.

Server User Password:
This field is for your password on the system where the server is running. If you supply a **Server User Name** without a **Server User Password**, then you will be prompted for a password at connection time.

7. When you have finished making any necessary changes to the Local DDE Options or TCP Options dialogs, select **OK** to return to the Servers page (Display 2.4).

8. **Important!** Select the **<<Add<<** button to save your server definition. The server name now appears in the list of defined servers at the left.

9. To define another server, repeat steps 2-8.

Deleting a Server Definition

To delete a previously defined server, do the following:

1. Select the server name from the **Servers** list at the left of the Servers page.

2. Select the **>>Remove>>** button.

▶ *Caution* . . . . *If you delete a server, then any data sources that use that server will no longer be accessible, until or unless you redefine that server.*

Modifying a Server Definition

To change the information for a previously defined server, do the following:

1. Select the server name from the **Servers** list at the left of the Servers page.

2. Make the desired changes to the **Password** and **Access Method** fields. Use the **Configure...** button to make changes in the Local DDE Options or TCP Options dialogs (Display 2.5 and Display 2.6).
    The **Name** field is greyed out to indicate that you cannot change the name of the server. The reason for this is that you may have already defined data sources that use that server; if you changed the server name, then you would no longer be able to access those data sources.

3. Select the **<<Update<<** button to save your changes.

For instructions on how to specify a different server for a data source that you have already defined, see "Specifying a Different Server for a Defined Data Source" on page 21.

Defining Data Libraries

Each data source can include multiple data libraries. (See page 5 for information about SAS data libraries.) Therefore, you provide information about each library that you want to access.
This section describes how to use the Libraries page to define your data libraries. See "Defining Libraries at Server Startup Time" on page 18 for information about an alternate way of defining data libraries.

1. Select the **Libraries** tab in the SAS ODBC Driver Configuration dialog to move the Libraries page to the foreground (Display 2.7). Supply the information described in the following steps. If at any point you want to clear all of the fields on the right side of the dialog and start again, select the **Clear** button in the upper right corner.

Display 2.7
Libraries Page

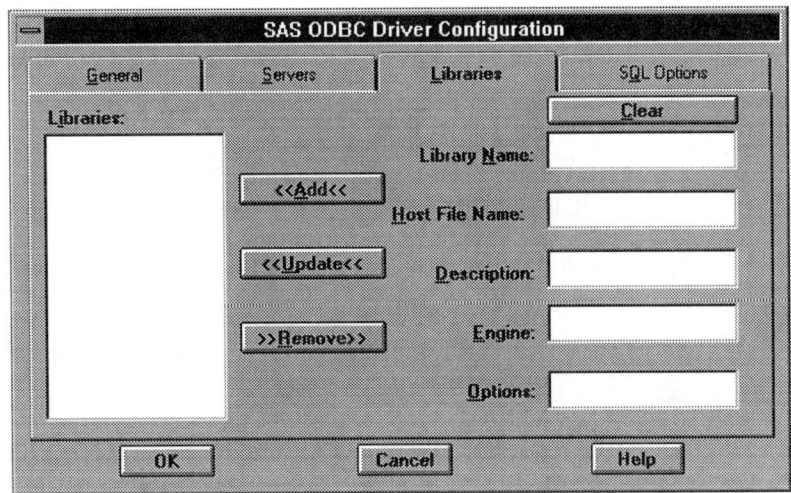

2. In the **Library Name** field, enter a name for an existing physical SAS data library that you want to access. (For those who are familiar with SAS, this field corresponds to the *libref* in the SAS LIBNAME statement.) The name can be up to eight characters long. The first character must be a letter or an underscore. Subsequent characters can be letters, numeric digits, or underscores. Blanks and special characters are not allowed. For example, you might use the name **cost** to designate a library of cost-accounting data.

   The SAS data library can include SAS data files, SAS data views, or both. See "SAS Data Sets" on page 3 for more information.

3. In the **Host File Name**, enter the physical name of the library. This must be a valid pathname for the operating system that your data library is stored on. For example, for a library that is stored on a PC in the Windows environment, **e:\fin\acct** would be a valid pathname.

4. (Optional:) In the **Description** field, supply a description of the library, to remind yourself or other users of what the library contains.

5. (Optional:) In the **Engine** field, enter the name of the SAS engine that is required for writing to and reading from this library. This is necessary only if you do not want the SAS server to use the default engine for the version and release number of the SAS System that you are running. (For Release 6.11 of the SAS System, the default engine would be **V611**.) For information about other engines that may be available, see the description of the LIBNAME statement in the SAS Companion for the operating system under which your data library is stored.

6. (Optional:) In the **Options** field, you may enter the following option for the library that you are defining:

   ACCESS=READONLY
     This option limits users to "read only" access to the SAS data sets in the library.

> **Note:** In order to honor this option, the SAS server through which the library is accessed must be running under one of the following releases of the SAS system:*
>
> □ For Release 6.08, maintenance level TS415 or later
>
> □ For Release 6.09, the second maintenance level or later
>
> □ Release 6.10 or later.

7. Select the **<<Add<<** button to save your library information. The Library Name is added to the Libraries list at the left.

8. To include another data library with your data source, repeat steps 2-7.

Defining Libraries at Server Startup Time

Server administrators may prefer to define SAS data libraries at server startup time rather than defining them through the SAS ODBC driver dialogs. Defining libraries at server startup time can make opening the data source faster. It also enables you to avoid hard-coding the physical names of your libraries in your SAS ODBC data-source definitions.

As explained in "SAS Servers" on page 5, the SAS ODBC driver uses a SAS/SHARE server (invoked by PROC SERVER) to access remote data sources. It uses a SAS ODBC server (invoked by PROC ODBCSERVER) to access local data sources. To define a data library at server startup time, you precede the PROC SERVER or PROC ODBCSERVER statement with a SAS LIBNAME statement. For example, you could define a library of cost-accounting data to a SAS/SHARE server as follows:

```
libname cost 'e:\fin\acct';
proc server id=acctserv;
run;
```

To define this library to a SAS ODBC server, you would add only the above LIBNAME statement to the !SASROOT\CORE\SASMACRO\SASODBC.SAS file. See the discussion of the **SAS Parameters** field on page 14 for more information.

When a user requests access to the particular SAS ODBC data source from an ODBC client application, the server would automatically make this library available, along with any libraries that were defined via the SAS ODBC Libraries page.

For more information about the SAS LIBNAME statement, see the SAS Companion for the operating system under which your data library is stored.

---

* This option was available with earlier releases on the SAS LIBNAME statement, but in the interface that is used by the SAS ODBC driver it has been supported only since the stated releases and maintenance levels.

Deleting a Data Library Definition

To delete a previously defined data library, do the following:

1. Select the library name from the **Libraries** list at the left of the Libraries page (Display 2.7).

2. Select the **>>Remove>>** button.

Modifying a Data Library Definition

To change the information for a previously defined library, do the following:

1. Select the library name from the **Libraries** list on the Libraries page.

2. Make the desired changes to the **Host File Name**, **Description**, **Engine**, and **Options** fields.

3. Select the **<<Update<<** button to save your changes.

Specifying SQL Options

SQL options affect the interaction between the SAS ODBC driver, SAS, and ODBC-compliant applications. The default settings for the options are those that most ODBC-compliant applications will expect and will work best with. However, you can override the defaults by selecting any of the items on the SQL Options page.

1. Select the **SQL Options** tab to move the SQL Options page to the foreground.

Display 2.8
SQL Options Page

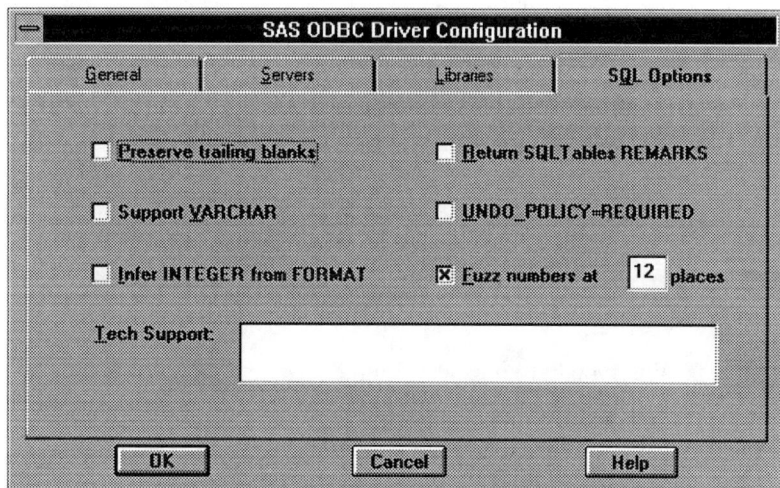

2. The options that the page contains are described on the next page. Click on the box to the left of any option that you want to specify. An 'X' appears in the box when the associated option has been selected. Select as many options as you want. To deselect an option, click on it again.

Preserve trailing blanks
> preserves trailing blanks at the end of character fields. The default action is that trailing blanks are removed, so that each field ends in a null.

Support VARCHAR
> causes character fields that are longer than 80 characters to be reported as variable-length fields, and causes the trailing blanks to be removed. See "Support VARCHAR Option" on page 37 for more information.

Infer INTEGER from FORMAT
> causes SAS numeric data types (typically reported as SQL_DOUBLE) to be reported as SQL_INTEGER. See "Infer INTEGER from FORMAT Option" on page 37 for more information.

Support SQLTables REMARKS
> causes the SAS ODBC driver to read and return the SAS data set label for each data set in the library you are accessing. (SQLTables is the name of an ODBC function that can be used for this purpose.) For SAS data sets, this can have a negative impact on performance, because each data set must be opened in order to read the label. Therefore, you should not select this option unless there is information in the label that you really need to see.

UNDO_POLICY=REQUIRED
> implements the UNDO_POLICY option of the SAS System's SQL procedure with a setting of REQUIRED. With this setting, INSERT or UPDATE operations that fail are undone. However, this action is performed only for operations that affect multiple records; a statement that affects a single record behaves the same regardless of the UNDO_POLICY setting. When UNDO_POLICY=REQUIRED, the associated **hstmt** of an UPDATE or INSERT statement must be the only active **hstmt** against the table. If another user, or an **hstmt** within the same user's application, has an active SELECT statement, the UPDATE or INSERT statement fails.

Fuzz Numbers at **N** Places
> specifies the degree of precision to use when comparing numbers. See "Fuzz Numbers at N Places Option" on page 37 for more information. By default, this option is selected. You can change the default value, 12, by typing over it.

Tech Support
> is for specifying options only as directed by SAS Institute Technical Support staff, if you require their assistance.

Saving Your Data Source Definition

When you have finished defining your data source, select **OK** to save your data source definition and return to the Data Sources dialog (Display 2.1). Your newly defined data source now appears in the list of Data Sources on the left.

You can either select **Add...** to define another data source, or select **Close** to return to the Microsoft Windows Control Panel (or to the location from which you entered the Data Sources dialog).

Modifying a Data Source Definition

To modify a previously defined data source, do the following:

1. Select the name of the data source from the Data Sources dialog (Display 2.1).

2. Select **Setup . . . .** The SAS ODBC Driver Configuration dialog (Display 2.3) appears.

3. Use the tabs in this dialog to access other SAS ODBC pages. Use the other pages as described in previous sections to modify server definitions, library definitions, or SQL options.

4. When you are finished, select **OK** to save your changes.

Specifying a Different Server for a Defined Data Source

Suppose that a data source named **Payroll** has been moved from a server named **CICERO** to one named **DAVINCI**. In this case, you need to change the server that you specified for the **Payroll** data source by doing the following:

1. Select the **Payroll** data source from the Data Sources dialog (Display 2.1).

2. Select **Setup . . . .** The SAS ODBC Driver Configuration dialog (Display 2.3) appears, with **CICERO** listed in the Servers field.

3. Use the Servers page to define the **DAVINCI** server, if it is not already defined.

4. From the General page, if **DAVINCI** is not already visible in the **Servers** field, select the drop-list icon next to that field, and then select **DAVINCI** from the list.

5. Select **OK** to save your changes.

Deleting a Data Source Definition

To delete a previously defined data source, do the following:

1. Select the name of the data source from the Data Sources dialog (Display 2.1).

2. Select **Delete**.

22

Chapter **3** Using the SAS® ODBC Driver

Introduction

This chapter provides an overview of how to use the SAS ODBC driver to access your SAS data sources, as well as information that may be important to some users. It also provides information about the SAS servers and the communications software that are used by the driver, and about SQL syntax and return codes that are supported by the driver.

Accessing Your Data Sources (Overview)

The details of how you access your SAS data sources depend on which ODBC-compliant Windows application you are using (for example, Microsoft Access or Excel), and on which communications software you use. However, here is an overview of the procedure that you follow:

1. Install the SAS ODBC driver. (Refer to the installation instructions that are shipped with the driver.) The installation program creates an icon if one does not already exist.

   □ In a Windows or Windows for Workgroups environment, the icon is labeled **ODBC** and is located in the Windows Control Panel.

   □ In a Windows NT environment, the icon is labeled **ODBC Administrator** and is located in the ODBC group.

   □ If you have already installed other ODBC drivers, then this icon was already created and your ODBC setup will be updated by the SAS ODBC driver installation program.

2. Double-click on the ODBC (or ODBC Administrator) icon to access the ODBC and SAS ODBC dialogs.

3. Use these dialogs to provide the SAS ODBC driver with the necessary information about your SAS data source(s). (See Chapter 2 for instructions.) In addition to SAS data files, SAS data sources can include DATA step views, PROC SQL views, or SAS/ACCESS views, all of which contain definitions of data that are stored elsewhere rather than the physical data itself. (See "What Kinds of Data Can I Access with the SAS ODBC Driver?" on page 2 and "SAS Data Sets" on page 3.)

4. The next step depends on whether you want to access local data or remote data and on which communications software you are using:

   □ To access local data sources using DDE (a form of interprocess communication that is part of the Windows operating environment), see "Using DDE as Your Local Access Method."
     Note: If you have not installed any other communications software on your PC and are accessing only local data sources, then DDE is the communications method that you must use.

   □ To access remote data sources using TCP/IP, see "Using TCP/IP as Your Remote Access Method" on page 25.

   □ To access remote data sources using Network DDE, see "Using Network DDE as Your Remote Access Method" on page 26.

5. Consult the documentation for your Windows application for instructions on how to access or import data from other sources. From the list of available data sources, select or specify the name that you assigned to your SAS data source.

6. Select or enter the name of the desired SAS data library (if required by your application).

7. Select or enter the name of the desired SAS data file or view.

Prerequisites for Various Communications Access Methods

The SAS ODBC driver interacts with other software to provide you with access to your data sources. Certain prerequisites apply, depending on the communications software you use and on whether you want to access local data or remote data. These prerequisites are described in the following sections.

Using DDE as Your Local Access Method

To access local SAS data sources, the SAS ODBC driver uses a SAS ODBC server in conjunction with DDE. (See page 5 for more information about SAS servers.) It is not necessary for the server to be running when you *define* your data sources. However, the server must be running on your PC in order for you to *access* your SAS data sources.

Starting a SAS ODBC Server

If there isn't already a SAS ODBC server running on your PC, the SAS ODBC driver uses the information that you supplied in the Local DDE Options dialog (Display 2.5, described on page 14) to automatically start one for you. That is, you do not need to take any action to start the server.

If you already have a SAS session running on your PC, then you can start the SAS ODBC server in that session by submitting the following statements:

```
options comamid=dde;
proc odbcserver id=server-name;
run;
```

The *server-name* must be the same as the name you specified in the Servers page when you defined your local data source, as explained in "Defining Servers" on page 12.

Alternatively, you can terminate your SAS session so that the SAS ODBC driver can start a SAS ODBC server for you in a new SAS session.*

Note: When the server is running in the SAS session, the SAS session does not accept user input from the keyboard.

If the SAS session cannot be started before the **SAS Timeout** value that you specified in the Local DDE Options dialog is reached, a timeout error is returned to your ODBC client application. An error message also is returned to the client if the SAS session was started but PROC ODBCSERVER could not execute.

Terminating the SAS ODBC Server

When you are finished using your ODBC client application to access your local SAS data sources, the SAS ODBC server continues to execute in case you may want to access additional SAS data sources. To terminate the server, do either of the following:

□ Open the Microsoft Windows Task List window by pressing the Ctrl and Escape keys simultaneously. Select **SAS** from the list of tasks, and then select the **End Task** button.

□ Bring the SAS session into focus (make it the active window), and then press the Ctrl and Break keys simultaneously. A dialog box asks you to confirm that you want to end your SAS server session. Select **OK**.

Using TCP/IP as Your Remote Access Method

To access remote data sources, the SAS ODBC driver uses a SAS/SHARE server. (See page 5 for more information about SAS servers. See the SAS/SHARE documentation, listed on page vii, for complete information about SAS/SHARE.) It is not necessary for the server to be running when you *define* your data sources. However, the server must be running on your remote host in order for you to *access* your data sources.

---

* Under Windows NT it is not necessary to terminate the SAS session, because you can run multiple SAS sessions in that environment.

Because a SAS/SHARE server is used by multiple users, it is usually invoked on the remote host at system startup time. Therefore, end users generally do not need to take any local action to invoke the server.

If you use TCP/IP as your communications access method, then you (or your server administrator) must do the following:

□ Specify **COMAMID=TCP** in an OPTIONS statement when you invoke PROC SERVER, as in the following example:

```
options comamid=tcp;
proc server id=server-name;
run;
```

□ Define your server(s) in the TCP/IP SERVICES file for your *client* machine(s).*

Each entry in the SERVICES file associates a service name with the port number and communications protocol that are used by that service. In this case, the service name that you use is the name of a SAS/SHARE server. An entry for a SAS/SHARE server has the form

```
<server-name>   <port number>/tcp   # <comments>
```

The server name must be 1-8 characters long, and it is generally case-sensitive. The first character must be a letter or an underscore; the remaining seven characters can include letters, digits, underscores, the dollar ($) sign, or the at (@) sign. You specify this same server name in the Servers page when you define your data source, as explained on page 12.

The entry must match the entry that is defined in the *server's* TCP/IP SERVICES file.

An entry for a server whose name is SALESERV might look like this:

```
saleserv          5000/tcp       # SAS server for Sales and Marketing
```

Using Network DDE as Your Remote Access Method

To access remote data sources, the SAS ODBC driver uses a SAS/SHARE server. (See page 5 for more information about SAS servers.) It is not necessary for the server to be running when you *define* your data sources. However, the server must be running on your remote host in order for you to *access* your data sources.

Because a SAS/SHARE server is used by multiple users, it is usually invoked on the remote host at system startup time. Therefore, end users generally do not need to take any local action to invoke the server.

However, if you use Network DDE as your communications software, then you must define the SAS/SHARE server as a Network DDE *share* in a Windows environment (such as Windows for Workgroups or Windows NT) that supports Network DDE. Both client and server machines must support Network DDE, but you define the share only on the server machine.

---

* Refer to the documentation for your TCP/IP software to find the path name for the SERVICES file.

The method of defining a Network DDE share depends on whether you use Windows NT or Windows for Workgroups. These methods are described in the following sections.

For more information about Network DDE, see the Windows for Workgroups Resource Kit Addendum for Version 3.11, the Windows NT Resource Kit, or the Microsoft Developers Network CD. The Microsoft Developers Network CD includes the Windows for Workgroups 3.11 Resource Kit.

Defining a Share under Windows NT

To define the share under Windows NT, use the DDESHARE.EXE program that is included with Windows NT. You must also define the share as a *trusted share*.

Example
Suppose you want to connect to a SAS/SHARE server named SHR1 on a networked DDE machine named GREENBAY. You would add a new share on the GREENBAY machine by doing the following:

1. Invoke the DDESHARE program on GREENBAY.

2. From the **Shares** menu, select **DDE Shares . . . .** The DDE Shares window appears.

3. Select the **Add a Share. . .** button. The DDE Share Properties window appears.

4. In the **Share Name** field, specify a name for the share. For example, you might use the name **SHR1$**. (By convention, DDE share names end with dollar signs).

5. Ignoring the Old Style and New Style rows, tab down to the Static row and enter **SHR1** as your Application Name. Be sure to use the same name that is specified for the ID= option in the PROC SERVER statement that you (or your server administrator) use to invoke the SAS/SHARE server on the remote host.

6. In the **Topic Name** field (still in the Static row), specify **SAS/SHARE**.

7. In the Item Security box, leave the **Grant access to all items** radio button selected.

8. Select the **Permissions. . .** button. The DDE Share Name Permissions window appears.

9. From the list of names, select **Everyone**.

10. From the scrollable Type of Access list, select **Full Control**.

11. Select **OK** to return to the DDE Share Properties window.

12. Select **OK** to return to the DDE Shares window.

To define a share as a trusted share, do the following:

1. From the DDE Shares window, select the share name that you just defined (**SHR1$**).

2. Select the **Trust Share. . .** button. The Trusted Share Properties window appears.

3. Select the boxes next to the **Start Application Enable** and **Initiate to Application Enable** items.

4. Select the **Set** button to save the properties.

5. Select **OK** to return to the DDE Shares window.

6. Select **OK** to exit from the DDESHARE program.

From your ODBC client machine, define the data sources that are stored on the GREENBAY machine (as described in Chapter 2). In the Servers page (Display 2.4, described on page 12), specify **GREENBAY.SHR1$** as the name of your server. **GREENBAY** specifies the remote machine name, and **SHR1$** specifies the DDE share name that you defined on the GREENBAY machine. Specify **DDE** as the access method.

Defining a Share under Windows for Workgroups: Preferred Method

To define the share under Windows for Workgroups, use the DDESHARE.EXE program. You can obtain this program from the Windows for Workgroups Resource kit.

Example

Suppose you want to connect to a SAS/SHARE server named SHR1 on a networked DDE machine named GREENBAY. You would add a new share on the GREENBAY machine by doing the following:

1. Invoke the DDESHARE program on GREENBAY. The Network DDE Share Manager window appears.

2. From the **Share** menu, select **New . . . .** The New Share window appears.

3. In the **Share Name** field, specify a name for the share. For example, you might use the name **SHR1$**. (By convention, DDE share names end with dollar signs).

4. In the **Application Name** field, specify **SHR1** as the name of your SAS/SHARE server. Be sure to use the same name that is specified for the ID= option in the PROC SERVER statement that you (or your server administrator) use to invoke the SAS/SHARE server on the remote host.

5. In the **Topic Name** field, specify **SAS/SHARE**. Do not specify an item name.

6. Select **Full** access type.

7. Select **OK** to exit from the DDESHARE program.

From your ODBC client machine, use the pages of the SAS ODBC Driver Configuration dialog (described in Chapter 2) to define data sources that are stored on the GREENBAY machine. In the Servers page (Display 2.4, described on page 12), specify **GREENBAY.SHR1$** as the name of your server. **GREENBAY** specifies the remote machine name, and **SHR1$** specifies the DDE share name that you defined on the GREENBAY machine. Specify **DDE** as the access method.

An Alternate Method of Defining a Share under Windows for Workgroups

Under Windows for Workgroups, you can also define a Network DDE share by updating the Windows SYSTEM.INI file instead of using the DDESHARE program. This method is not recommended, because the format of the SYSTEM.INI file may change, or some of its entries might be moved to other files in future versions of Microsoft Windows. However, if you do not have ready access to the DDESHARE program, you may want to use this method.

Using the same example of defining a share on a server machine named GREENBAY, you would add the following statement to the **[ddeshares]** section of the SYSTEM.INI file.

```
SHR1$=SHR1,SAS/SHARE,,15,,0,,0,0,0
```

This file would be located in the Windows system directory on the GREENBAY machine.

This statement tells Network DDE that the DDE share name **SHR1$** corresponds to the SAS/SHARE server that is registered as **SHR1** using the topic name **SAS/SHARE**. For the DDE application name, be sure to use the same name that is specified for the ID= option on the PROC SERVER statement that you (or your server administrator) use to invoke the SAS/SHARE server on the remote host.

The syntax of the remainder of this statement (beyond the **SAS/SHARE** topic name) is not documented by Microsoft. However, the statement shown above works fine for SAS/SHARE servers.

Other Important Usage Information

The information in this section may be important to some users. You should skim through this section to determine whether any of this information is relevant to you.

Using Data Sets That Have One-Level Names

If you use an ODBC application such as Microsoft Access that exports databases using one-level names, you should use the ODBC administrator to define a USER library. The SAS System normally places any data set that has a one-level name into the WORK library, which is deleted at the end of the SAS session. But if a USER library has been defined, SAS places all one-level name data sets into the USER library, which is saved at the end of the SAS session. In a multi-user environment, multiple client connections to a SAS System server can each have their own USER library defined.

Updating Attached Tables

Some Microsoft products that are based on the JET engine (such as Microsoft Access) have certain requirements in order to be able to update database tables. This may be true of other ODBC applications as well. These requirements may make it necessary for you to specify two SQL options when you define your SAS data sources.

□ The attached table must have a unique primary key that is not a floating-point value. You can use the Data Source SQL Option **Infer INTEGER from FORMAT** to indicate that SAS numeric fields without fractional parts (for example, FORMAT(n,0) where n is less than 12) are actually integer values that can be used to index the table.

□ All of the values in a row may be used to uniquely select the row for updating. This can be a problem in rows that contain floating-point fields (SAS numerics). Insignificant differences in values can be caused either by differences in floating-point representation on different machines or by conversion between character and binary formats. By specifying the Data Source SQL Option `Fuzz Numbers at 12 places`, you can cause WHERE clauses to select values that are "acceptably close" rather than requiring exact comparisons.

See "Specifying SQL Options" on page 19 and "User-Specified SQL Options" on page 36 for more information about these SQL options.

Using SQL Statements to Access SAS Data Sources

All ODBC-compliant applications use a variety of the Structured Query Language (SQL) to access and manipulate data. However, most of these applications transform user actions into SQL statements so that users themselves do not need to know anything about SQL.

If your application requires you to use SQL statements, or if you use SQL out of personal preference, then you should refer to *SAS Guide to the SQL Procedure: Usage and Reference.* The elements of SQL grammar that are supported by the SAS ODBC driver are the same as those described in that book.

Accessing the SAS Libraries MAPS, SASUSER, and SASHELP

By default, every SAS session (including SAS server sessions) provides access to the SAS libraries MAPS, SASUSER, and SASHELP. However, because these libraries contain sample data sets and other files that are generally not of interest to ODBC users, the SAS ODBC driver does not report the contents of these libraries when it invokes a SAS ODBC server. * If you want information from these libraries, you can do either of the following:

□   Use a LIBNAME statement to define the desired SAS library to the server.

□   Use the SAS ODBC Driver Configuration dialogs to define the desired library to your ODBC applications.

In both cases you must use a different name (that is, not MAPS, SASUSER, or SASHELP) as your libref or library name.

Return Codes and Associated Messages

The SAS ODBC driver uses standard ODBC return codes to notify you of any errors and to provide additional information or warnings. The associated message texts may be generated by the driver itself, by the SAS server, or by your communications access method. See the *Microsoft ODBC 2.0 Programmer's Reference and SDK Guide* and the Appendix in this report for explanations of these return codes and their associated texts.

---

*   From a programming standpoint, when SQLTables, SQLStatistics, or SQLColumns is called, the result set that is returned does not include rows for the SAS libraries MAPS, SASUSER, or SASHELP.

Chapter 4 Programmer's Reference

Introduction

This chapter is intended for applications programmers and others who need information about how the SAS ODBC driver has been implemented. It provides information about the driver's support for ODBC functions, SQL grammar, and SQL data types.

For complete information about the ODBC standard, see the *Microsoft ODBC 2.0 Programmer's Reference and SDK Guide.*

Support for and Implementation of ODBC Functions

Microsoft's ODBC specification defines three levels of support for ODBC functions: CORE, LEVEL 1, and LEVEL 2. The SAS ODBC driver supports LEVEL 1 functionality, with the exception of those functions associated with cursors (SQLGetCursorName, SQLSetCursorName) and large data fields (SQLParamData, SQLPutData). The following tables provide explanations of the functions that are not supported or whose implementation details may be noteworthy to applications developers.

CORE Functions

Function Name	Purpose	SAS ODBC Driver Implementation
SQLBindParameter	Assigns storage for a parameter in an SQL statement	Note that SQL_DATA_AT_EXEC is not supported because SAS does not support large data fields.
SQLCancel	Cancels an SQL statement	This function is used only in asynchronous mode, which SAS does not support. The SAS System's interprocess communication library does not provide any way to interrupt a transaction in process. SQLCancel does not cause an active statement to terminate immediately, and it does not halt an operation that is already in process. This is allowable within the function specification. This call always returns as successful.
SQLColAttributes	Describes the attributes of a column in the result set	A common reason for applications to call this function is to determine whether a column of data is a dollar amount. With SAS data sets or views, this is inferred from the FORMAT. See "Supported Data Types" on page 34 for more information about SAS FORMATs.
SQLGetCursorName	Returns the cursor name that is associated with a statement handle	SAS does not support cursors, so this function returns SQL_ERROR with SQLSTATE set to IM001 ("Driver does not support this function").
SQLPrepare	Prepares an SQL statement for later execution	Does not check syntax at this point; syntax checking is done later in the SQLExecute call by the server.
SQLSetCursorName	Specifies a cursor name	SAS does not support cursors, so this function returns SQL_ERROR with SQLSTATE set to IM001 ("Driver does not support this function").
SQLTransact	Commits or rolls back a transaction	Always returns SQL_SUCCESS for SQL_COMMIT. Returns an error for SQL_ROLLBACK because SAS does not support transactions.

LEVEL 1 Functions

Function Name	Purpose	SAS ODBC Driver Implementation
SQLColumns	Returns the list of column names from specified tables	SAS uses a specially formatted query to query the virtual table DICTIONARY.COLUMNS.
SQLDriverConnect	Connects to a specific driver by connection string or requests that the Driver Manager and the driver display connection dialogs for the user	SAS makes use of the same dialogs that are used in configuration. If input was adequate, it continues with the connection rather than saving the parameters. However, in many cases input is not required. The connection to the host is made at this time.
SQLParamData	Returns the storage value that has been assigned to a parameter for which data will be sent at execution time	This function is used for large data fields, which SAS does not support, so the function returns SQL_ERROR with SQLSTATE set to IM001 ("Driver does not support this function").
SQLPutData	Sends part or all of a data value for a parameter	This function is used for large data fields, which SAS does not support, so the function returns SQL_ERROR with SQLSTATE set to IM001 ("Driver does not support this function").
SQLSpecialColumns	Retrieves information about the optimal set of columns that uniquely identifies a row in a specified table, or about the columns that are automatically updated when any value in the row is updated by a transaction	The SAS ODBC driver uses a query on the DICTIONARY.INDEXES view to obtain this information.
SQLStatistics	Retrieves statistics about a single table and the list of indexes that are associated with the table	The SAS ODBC driver uses a query on the DICTIONARY.INDEXES view to obtain this information.
SQLTables	Returns the list of table names stored in a specific data source	The SAS ODBC driver uses a query on the DICTIONARY.TABLES and DICTIONARY.MEMBERS views to obtain this information.

Support for SQL Grammar

Microsoft's ODBC specification defines three levels of support for SQL grammar: MINIMUM, CORE and EXTENDED. The SAS ODBC driver supports all of MINIMUM and some of CORE for SQL statements and for the elements that are used in those statements. See *SAS Guide to the SQL Procedure: Usage and Reference* for complete information about supported grammar.

Supported Data Types

Internally, the SAS System supports two data types for storing data:

CHAR   fixed-length character data, 200-character maximum

NUM   double-precision floating-point number

However, by using SAS *format* information, the SAS ODBC driver is able to represent other ODBC data types, both when responding to queries and in CREATE TABLE requests. (A SAS format is a string that describes how data should be printed. The SAS System associates format information with each column in a table.)

The following sections explain conventions for data type representation that the SAS ODBC driver follows.

For information about user-specified SQL options that can also affect data type representations, see "User-Specified SQL Options" on page 36. For more information about SAS formats, see *SAS Language: Reference, Version 6, First Edition.*

Data Types Reported on Queries

When the SQLDescribeCol and SQLColAttributes functions are called against active queries, the SAS ODBC driver reports data types as follows:

□   When the SQLDescribeCol function is called, the SAS ODBC driver reports CHAR data types as SQL_CHAR. NUM data types are generally reported as SQL_DOUBLE.
    However, the SAS System stores dates and times as numbers, and the SAS ODBC driver uses SAS format information to infer the following additional SQL data types from NUM data types:*

SAS Data Type	SQL Data Type
NUM FORMAT=DATE*n*.	SQL_DATE
NUM FORMAT=TIME*n*.	SQL_TIME
NUM FORMAT=DATETIME*n*.	SQL_TIMESTAMP

---

*   For a complete list of date and time formats that the SAS ODBC driver supports, see the table of formats listed by categories on page 68 of *SAS Language: Reference, Version 6, First Edition.*

In each of the previous FORMAT= strings, *n* is a number that selects the printable representation by specifying a width for printing. The value of *n* is not relevant to the driver.

□ When the SQLColAttributes function is called, if a NUM column has a format of DOLLAR*n*., the SAS ODBC driver identifies it as financial data (having a column attribute of SQL_COLUMN_MONEY).

Creating or Comparing Date, Time, and Datetime Values

When you create or compare date, time and datetime values in SAS data sets from an ODBC application, you must consider the following:

□ A SAS time value is the number of seconds since the current day began. That is, 0 is 00:00:00 or 12:00:00 AM and 86399 is 11:59:59 PM)
   Note: ODBC does not support negative time values or values greater than one day's worth of seconds. The SAS ODBC driver returns an error for time values that are less than 0 or greater than 86399 (the last second of the day).

□ A SAS date value is the number of days since January 1, 1960. That is, 0 is 01jan1960 and -1 is 31dec1959).

□ A SAS datetime value is the number of seconds since midnight on January 1, 1960. That is, 0 is 01jan1960:00:00:00 and -1 is 31dec1959:11:59:59)

Both ODBC and SAS date, time and datetime literals are supported by the SAS ODBC Driver.

▶ *Caution* . . . . *You can only compare equivalent literals against SAS date, time or datetime values since they each have a different unit of measure.*

For example, you cannot compare a SAS data set value that has been defined with a datetime format against a date literal using

```
    select * where hiredate = {d'1995-01-02'}
or
    select * where hiredate = '02jan1995'd
```

Instead, use a datetime literal such as

```
    select * where hiredate = {ts'1995-01-02 00:00:00'}
or
    select * where hiredate = '02jan1995:00:00:00'dt
```

Interpretation of Data Types in CREATE TABLE Requests

In CREATE TABLE requests, the SAS ODBC driver interprets certain column-type specifications by creating NUM variables and associating SAS formats with them, as shown in the following table:

Table 4.1
Correspondence of
CREATE TABLE
Data Types and SAS
Data Types

CREATE TABLE Data Type Name	ODBC Data Type	SAS Data Type
char(*w*)	SQL_CHAR	CHAR(*w*)
num(*w,d*)	SQL_DOUBLE	NUM
num(*w,d*)	SQL_FLOAT	NUM
integer	SQL_INTEGER	NUM FORMAT=11.0
date9x	SQL_DATE	NUM FORMAT=DATE9.
datetime19x	SQL_TIMESTAMP	NUM FORMAT=DATETIME19.
time8x	SQL_TIME	NUM FORMAT=TIME8X.

The data type names listed in the first column of the table are the values that are returned by SQLColAttributes (with the parameter SQL_COLUMN_TYPE_NAME) and by SQLGetTypeInfo. For all CREATE TABLE statements, the SAS ODBC driver translates these data type names into the respective SAS data types shown under the SAS Data Type heading. Do not try to use the ODBC data types directly in SAS.

In a CREATE TABLE statement, any FORMAT= specification is passed on to the SAS System unmodified, so a column within a table (or data set) can be created according to any exact specification that is required for its use within SAS. For example, in the following CREATE TABLE statement, variable **B**'s data type and format are passed directly to the SAS System.

```
CREATE TABLE
    SASUSER.TABLE1
        (A INTEGER,
         B NUM FORMAT=9.5,
         C CHAR(40) );
```

User-Specified SQL Options

This section describes two SQL options that affect how other default conversions of data types or data values can be made: **Infer INTEGER from FORMATS** and **Support VARCHAR**. A third SQL option, **Fuzz Numbers at N Places**, is important in comparison operations. You can specify these options in the SQL Options page of the SAS ODBC Driver Configuration dialog. (See "Specifying SQL Options" on page 19.)

Infer INTEGER from FORMAT Option

Even when no FORMAT string is specified for SAS data, the SAS System assigns a default width and number of decimal places to the data. If the SQL Option **Infer INTEGER from FORMAT** is selected, then the SAS ODBC driver reports SAS columns of NUM(n,0) data types as SQL_INTEGER, where n is less than 12. This can be important, because some PC products do not use indexes on floating-point columns. If those columns actually contain only integer values, then using this option enables these products to honor the index and to allow updates. See "Updating Attached Tables" on page 29 for more information.

Support VARCHAR Option

The SQL option **Support VARCHAR** causes the SAS ODBC driver to report the data type CHAR(n) as SQL_VARCHAR, where n is greater than 80. Because SAS is fixed width, CHAR fields are often specified at the maximum. For example, for a list of messages the text width might be specified as 200 characters, even though the average width is much less. Reporting it as SQL_VARCHAR enables some PC products to use less memory.

Fuzz Numbers at N Places Option

This option addresses a problem that arises from the conversion of floating-point numbers. Floating-point numbers are stored in different binary representations on different computer hardware. Even when data are transferred between different applications on the same type of hardware, the precision of floating-point numbers may be affected slightly due to conversion between ASCII and binary representations.

This effect is usually so slight that it is insignificant when a number is used in calculations. For example, the numbers 65.8 and 65.799999999999 are practically identical for mathematical purposes, and the difference between them might be the result of conversion between representations rather than any purposeful change in value.

However, such a slight difference in value can keep a number from comparing correctly. For example, many ODBC applications include a WHERE clause that lists every column in a record at its current value whenever the application performs an UPDATE. This is done to ensure that the record has not been changed since the last time it was read. Sometimes a comparison may fail because of the aforementioned problem with floating-point conversion.

To solve this problem, SAS "fuzzes" numbers (standardizes the degree of precision to use, overriding the hardware-specific representations). Instead of using exact comparisons, SAS checks to make sure that the numbers are acceptably close.

By default, the degree of precision is 12 decimal places. Given a number **N**, then if **N1** were to be checked for equality with **N**, the SAS ODBC driver would use the SQL BETWEEN function to determine whether **N1 > (N - (ABS(N * 10**-12))) AND N1 < (N + (ABS(N * 10**-12)))**.

If **N=0**, the driver checks for **BETWEEN -(10**-12) AND (10**-12)**.

SAS ODBC Driver Error Codes

See the *Microsoft ODBC 2.0 Programmer's Reference and SDK Guide* for information about the SQLSTATE values (return codes) and associated texts that can be returned for the SQLError function.

For explanations of message texts that may be returned by your communications software, see the Appendix in this report.

Appendix Return Codes and Associated Messages

SAS ODBC Driver Return Codes

See the *Microsoft ODBC 2.0 Programmer's Reference and SDK Guide* for information about the SQLSTATE values (return codes) and the associated texts that can be returned for the SQLError function. The message texts may be generated by the driver itself, by the SAS server, or by your communications software. The ODBC Driver Manager passes these codes and messages on to client applications.

S1000 Communications Access Method Errors

The S1000 (SAS API Error) return code is often accompanied by error messages that are returned by your communications software. The following tables list some of these message texts and provide explanations for them.

In addition to these error messages and return codes, some additional information can sometimes be found in a "trace" file that is created in the working directory of the ODBC client application that fails a connection to a SAS server. This trace file has the name **WQExxxxx.TRC**, where *xxxxx* is the process ID of the ODBC client application at the time of failure.

Table A.1 S1000 Communication Access Method Errors

Message Text	Explanation
DDE method API <*function-name*> failed with DdeGetLastError <*rc*>	A DDEML return code (*rc*) was returned. Even though it is impossible to document all the possible reasons one might get one of these return codes, they are listed in Table A.2 to provide some indication of where the DDEML transport is having a problem.
Memory failure	Not enough memory is available.
Network failure	An unspecified network failure occurred.
No server found	The remote server was not found.
Remote closed connection	The SAS server disconnected.
Remote refused connection	The remote system disallowed a connection. Check the remote services file.

(continued)

Table A.1 *(continued)*

Message Text	Explanation
Start SAS failure - please check your SAS server parameters	The ShellExecute statement failed when starting SAS. Check to see whether the SAS paths are specified properly.
TCP method Winsock API *<function-name>* failed with WSAGetLastError *<rc>*	A TCP/IP Winsock return code (*rc*) was returned. Even though it is impossible to document all the possible reasons one might get one of these return codes, they are listed in Table A.3 to provide some indication of where the Winsock transport is having a problem.
Timeout waiting for the SAS server - check the startup options	A SAS server did not register itself as a DDE server within the specified time period.
Unable to locate remote host	TCP/IP could not find the remote host name.
Unable to locate service	TCP/IP could not find the server name in the services file.
Userid.password security failure	User ID and password verification failed on the remote machine.
You must connect to SAS/SHARE on a remote machine	You must select the SAS/SHARE button in the SAS ODBC Servers page (Display 2.4) in order to connect to a remote machine.

DDEML Return Codes

The documentation for version 3.1 of the Windows Software Development Kit (SDK) states only which of the Dynamic Data Exchange Management Library (DDEML) error values can be returned to each of the API functions. No descriptions of the different error values are included. (Descriptions *are* included in the Win32 SDK documentation.) The following list describes each of the possible error codes that can be returned by the DDEML, its corresponding value, and a description of what may have caused the error.

Table A.2 *DDEML Return Codes*

Return Code	Return-Code Mnemonic	Description
0x4000	DMLERR_ADVACKTIMEOUT	A synchronous transaction attempt has timed out.
0x4001	DMLERR_BUSY	The response to the transaction caused the DDE_FBUSY bit to be set.
0x4002	DMLERR_DATAACKTIMEOUT	A synchronous transaction attempt has timed out.
0x4003	DMLERR_DLL_NOT_INITIALIZED	A DDEML API was called without first calling the DdeInitialize function, or an invalid IdInst parameter was passed to an API.
0x4004	DMLERR_DLL_USAGE	An application initialized as a MONITOR has attempted DDE transactions, or an application initialized as CLIENTONLY has attempted SERVER transactions.

(continued)

Table A.2 *(continued)*

Return Code	Return-Code Mnemonic	Description
0x4005	DMLERR_EXECACKTIMEOUT	A synchronous transaction attempt has timed out.
0x4006	DMLERR_INVALIDPARAMETER	A parameter failed validation. Some of the possible causes are as follows:
		• The application used a data handle initialized with a different hszItem than that required by the transaction.
		• The application used a data handle initialized with a different wFmt than that required by the transaction.
		• The application used a client-side hConv with a server-side API or vice versa.
		• The application used a freed data handle or hsz handle.
		• More than one instance of the application used the same object.
0x4007	DMLERR_LOW_MEMORY	This error happens only in an XTYP_ERROR callback, generally after a prolonged race condition (where the server application outruns the client) that consumes huge amounts of memory.
0x4008	DMLERR_MEMORY_ERROR	A memory allocation failed.
0x4009	DMLERR_NOTPROCESSED	A transaction failed — generally with a NACK.
0x400a	DMLERR_NO_CONV_ESTABLISHED	A connection attempt failed to receive an ACK in reply.
0x400b	DMLERR_POKEACKTIMEOUT	A synchronous transaction attempt has timed out.
0x400c	DMLERR_POSTMSG_FAILED	An internal PostMessage call failed.
0x400d	DMLERR_REENTRANCY	A synchronous transaction was initiated while the application instance has another synchronous transaction in progress, or the DdeEnableCallback function was called from within a callback.
0x400e	DMLERR_SERVER_DIED	A synchronous transaction was initiated while the application instance has another synchronous transaction in progress, or the DdeEnableCallback function was called from within a callback.
0x400f	DMLERR_SYS_ERROR	A system API failed inside of the DDEML.
0x4010	DMLERR_UNADVACKTIMEOUT	A synchronous transaction attempt has timed out.
0x4011	DMLERR_UNFOUND_QUEUE_ID	An invalid transaction ID was passed to an API function. Once the application has returned from an XTYP_XACT_COMPLETE callback, the transaction ID for that callback is no longer valid.

TCP/IP Winsock Return Codes

Table A.3 *TCP/IP Winsock Return Codes*

Return Code	Return-Code Mnemonic	Description
10004	WSAEINTR	The (blocking) call was canceled via WSACancelBlockingCall.
10013	WSAEACCES	The requested address is a broadcast address, but the appropriate flag was not set.
10014	WSAEFAULT	The function argument is incorrect.
10022	WSAEINVAL	Invalid argument or function sequence or the socket has not been bound with bind.
10024	WSAEMFILE	No more file descriptors are available.
10035	WSAEWOULDBLOCK	The socket is marked as non-blocking and the operation would block.
10036	WSAEINPROGRESS	A blocking Windows Sockets call is in progress.
10037	WSAEALREADY	The asynchronous routine being canceled has already completed.
10038	WSAENOTSOCK	The descriptor is not a socket.
10039	WSAEDESTADDREQ	A destination address is required.
10040	WSAEMSGSIZE	The datagram was too large to fit into the specified buffer and was truncated.
10041	WSAEPROTOTYPE	The specified protocol is the wrong type for this socket.
10042	WSAENOPROTOOPT	The option is unknown or unsupported.
10043	WSAEPROTONOSUPPORT	The specified protocol is not supported.
10044	WSASOCKTNOSUPPORT	The specified socket type is not supported in this address family.
10045	WSAEOPNOTSUPP	The referenced socket is not the proper type.
10046	WSAEPFNOSUPPORT	The protocol family is not supported.
10047	WSAEAFNOSUPPORT	The specified address family is not supported.
10048	WSAEADDRINUSE	The specified address is already in use.
10049	WSAEADDRNOTAVAIL	The specified address is not available from the local machine.
10050	WSAENETDOWN	The Windows Sockets implementation has detected that the network subsystem has failed.
10051	WSAENETUNREACH	The network can't be reached from this host at this time.

(continued)

Table A.3 *(continued)*

Return Code	Return-Code Mnemonic	Description
10052	WSAENETRESET	The connection must be reset because the Windows Sockets implementation dropped it.
10053	WSAECONNABORTED	The virtual circuit was aborted due to timeout or other failure.
10054	WSAECONNRESET	The virtual circuit was reset by the remote side.
10055	WSAENOBUFS	No buffer space is available.
10056	WSAEISCONN	The socket is already connected.
10057	WSAENOTCONN	The socket is not connected.
10058	WSAESHUTDOWN	The socket has been shutdown.
10059	WSAETOOMANYREFS	Too many references: can't splice.
10060	WSAETIMEDOUT	Attempt to connect timed out without establishing a connection.
10061	WSAECONNREFUSED	The attempt to connect was forcefully rejected.
10062	WSAELOOP	Too many levels of symbolic links.
10063	WSAENAMETOOLONG	The filename is too long.
10064	WSAEHOSTDOWN	The host is down.
10065	WSAEHOSTUNREACH	No route to host.
10066	WSAENOTEMPTY	The directory is not empty.
10067	WSAEPROCLIM	Too many processes.
10068	WSAEUSERS	Too many users.
10069	WSAEQUOT	The disk quota was exceeded.
10070	WSAESTALE	Stale NFS file handle.
10071	WSAEREMOTE	Too many levels of remote in path.
10091	WSAESYSNOTREADY	The underlying network subsystem is not ready for network communication.
10092	WSASVERNOTSUPPORTED	The version of Windows Sockets API support requested is not provided by this particular Windows Sockets implementation.
10093	WSANOTINITIALISED	A successful WSAStartup must occur before using this API.
11001	WSAHOST_NOT_FOUND	Authoritative Answer Host not found.
11002	WSATRY_AGAIN	Non-Authoritative Host not found, or SERVERFAIL.
11003	WSANO_RECOVERY	Non recoverable errors, FORMERR, REFUSED, NOTIMP.
11004	WSANO_DATA	Valid name, no data record of requested type.

Glossary

access descriptor
a SAS/ACCESS file that describes to the SAS System data that are in a database management system (DBMS) table or in a PC file. You use an access descriptor as a master descriptor file from which to create view descriptors. See also view and view descriptor.

access method
the communications protocol that the SAS ODBC driver uses to exchange data with a SAS server. The driver currently supports the use of TCP/IP and Network DDE for remote data exchange, and DDE for local data exchange.

application programming interface (API)
a set of software functions that facilitate communication between applications and other kinds of programs or services.

API
See application programming interface (API).

client
a computer or application that requests services, data, or other resources from a server. See also server.

database management system (DBMS)
an integrated software package that enables you to create and manipulate data in the form of databases.

DBMS
See database management system (DBMS).

DDE
See Dynamic Data Exchange (DDE).

dialog window
a window that prompts a user for additional information in order to perform a specified action.

driver
See ODBC driver.

Dynamic Data Exchange (DDE)
a standard mechanism in the PC environment for sharing data among applications. See also Network DDE.

engine
a part of the SAS System that reads from or writes to a file. Each engine enables the SAS System to access files that have a particular format.

libref
the name that is temporarily associated with a SAS data library. For example, in the name SASUSER.ACCOUNTS, the name SASUSER is the libref. To assign a libref, you use either the SAS LIBNAME statement or your operating system control language.

local data

data that are accessed through a SAS server on your PC. The data may be stored either on your PC hard drive or on a network file system, such as a Novell file server, that makes the physical location of the data transparent to applications.

Network DDE

an implementation of the DDE protocol over a network. (See Dynamic Data Exchange (DDE.)) Network DDE is supported by Microsoft's Windows for Workgroups and Windows NT.

ODBC driver

a loadable library module that provides a standardized interface to disparate databases or data sources.

remote data

data that are accessed through a SAS server that is running on another machine.

SAS server

a SAS session that provides other SAS sessions with access to SAS data sets, including SAS/ACCESS view descriptors. See also view descriptor.

server

a computer or application that is reserved for servicing other computers or applications. Servers can provide file services and communication services, and they enable users to access common resources such as disks, data, and modems. See also client.

TCP/IP

an abbreviation for a pair of networking protocols. Transmission Control Protocol (TCP) is a standard protocol for transferring information on local area networks such as Ethernets. TCP ensures that process-to-process information is delivered in the proper order. Internet Protocol (IP) is a protocol for managing connections between hosts. IP routes information through the network to a particular host, and fragments and reassembles information in host-to-host transfers.

view

a definition of a virtual data set. The definition is named and stored for later use. This file contains no data but describes or defines data that are stored elsewhere. See also view descriptor.

view descriptor

a SAS/ACCESS file that defines all or a subset of the database management system (DBMS) data or PC file data that are described by an access descriptor. See also access descriptor.

Index

Your Turn

If you have comments or suggestions about *SAS ODBC Driver Technical Report: User's Guide and Programmer's Reference, Release 6.11*, please send them to us on a photocopy of this page or send us electronic mail.

For comments about this book, please return the photocopy to

> SAS Institute Inc.
> Publications Division
> SAS Campus Drive
> Cary, NC 27513
> **email:** yourturn@unx.sas.com

For suggestions about the software, please return the photocopy to

> SAS Institute Inc.
> Technical Support Division
> SAS Campus Drive
> Cary, NC 27513
> **email:** suggest@unx.sas.com